T0387214

HOW DO OBJECTS MOVE?

LAURA L. SULLIVAN

Cavendish
Square
New York

Published in 2019 by Cavendish Square Publishing, LLC
243 5th Avenue, Suite 136, New York, NY 10016

Copyright © 2019 by Cavendish Square Publishing, LLC

First Edition

No part of this publication may be reproduced, stored in a retrieval system, or transmitted in any form or by any means–electronic, mechanical, photocopying, recording, or otherwise–without the prior permission of the copyright owner. Request for permission should be addressed to Permissions, Cavendish Square Publishing, 243 5th Avenue, Suite 136, New York, NY 10016. Tel (877) 980-4450; fax (877) 980-4454.

Website: cavendishsq.com

This publication represents the opinions and views of the author based on his or her personal experience, knowledge, and research. The information in this book serves as a general guide only. The author and publisher have used their best efforts in preparing this book and disclaim liability rising directly or indirectly from the use and application of this book.

All websites were available and accurate when this book was sent to press.

Library of Congress Cataloging-in-Publication Data

Names: Sullivan, Laura L., 1974- author.
Title: How do objects move? / Laura L. Sullivan.
Description: First edition. | New York : Cavendish Square Publishing, [2019] | Series: How does it move? Forces and motion | Includes bibliographical references and index. | Audience: 2-5.
Identifiers: LCCN 2017048029 (print) | LCCN 2017059703 (ebook) | ISBN 9781502637666 (ebook) | ISBN 9781502637642 (library bound) | ISBN 9781502637659 (pbk.) | ISBN 9781502639943 (6 pack) Subjects: LCSH: Motion--Juvenile literature.
Classification: LCC QC133.5 (ebook) | LCC QC133.5 .S84 2019 (print) | DDC 531/.11--dc23
LC record available at https://lccn.loc.gov/2017048029

Editorial Director: David McNamara
Editor: Fletcher Doyle/Meghan Lamb
Copy Editor: Michele Suchomel–Casey
Associate Art Director: Amy Greenan
Designer: Alan Sliwinski
Production Coordinator: Karol Szymczuk
Photo Research: J8 Media

The photographs in this book are used by permission and through the courtesy of: Cover Hero Images/Getty Images; p. 4 ©iStockphoto.com/skynesher; p. 6 Designua/Shutterstock.com; p. 7 Stockbyte/Thinkstock; p. 8 mTaira/Shutterstock.com; p. 9 Roman Sigaev/Shutterstock.com; p. 10 Africa Studio/Shutterstock.com; p. 12 ©iStockphoto.com/franckreporter; p. 13 Reji/Shutterstock.com; p. 14 Viktor Drachev/AFP/Getty Images; p. 15 Amy Myers/Shutterstock.com; p. 17 Lorelyn Medina/Shutterstock.com; p. 18 NASA/Getty Images; p. 19 ©iStockphoto.com/wanderluster; p. 20 Musee des Beaux-Arts, Rouen,France/Bridgeman Images; p. 22 Science Source/Getty Images; p. 23 De Agostini Picture Library/Getty Images; p. 24 Imagno/Hulton Fine Art Collection/Getty Images; p. 25 Keystone-France/Gamma-Keystone/Getty Images; p. 26 Getty Images.

Printed in the United States of America

CONTENTS

The world around you is in constant motion.

CHAPTER 1

EVERYTHING IS MOVING

E verything around us is in motion. Sometimes we can't see the movement. You might be alone in an empty room sitting still. Even then, the **molecules** inside your body are moving. The air is moving. Solid things that look perfectly still have **atoms** that vibrate.

MOVING OBJECTS

Most objects in motion are on a bigger scale. You walk to school. Your mother drives her car. Your sister throws a football.

All of these objects have **mass**. Mass is the amount of matter in something. Mass is different than **weight**. An object's mass stays the same. It doesn't change in different locations. Weight can change because it depends on **gravity**.

Low density

High density

The blue balls stand for mass. Objects with more mass weigh more.

WHAT IS MOVEMENT?

Movement is a change in position. Things move because a **force** is applied to them. A force is something that causes a change of motion in an object.

When you push someone on a swing, you apply force. Forces can make objects move. Forces can also slow down objects or stop them.

STUDYING MOTION

There are three main laws that explain how objects move. They are called Newton's laws of motion.

Applying force to someone on a swing makes them move.

Sir Isaac Newton was a scientist and mathematician. He lived more than three hundred years ago. The first law says that objects don't move (or change their motion) unless an outside force acts on them. The second law states that the force of an object depends on its mass and its **acceleration**. Acceleration is the change in speed

You use Newton's laws of motion every time you play a sport.

of an object. It can mean speeding up or slowing down. The third law says that for every action, there is an equal

STIRRING UP ATOMS

A metal spoon looks solid, but each of its atoms is vibrating. Heat makes atoms move faster. If you stir hot soup, the spoon's atoms will move more quickly. When the atoms move faster, the spoon will get hot.

and opposite reaction. When a bowling ball collides with a pin, each object feels the force of the other. The ball will slow down a little because of the force of the pin. The ball has more mass than the

Molecules inside objects move faster when they are hot.

pin. It is also moving. This gives it more force. The pin will move a lot when hit by the ball. The ball gives the pin acceleration.

A soccer game shows all three of Newton's laws of motion.

CHAPTER 2

BALLS IN MOTION

We use the laws of **physics** all the time. Usually, we don't even think about it. But every time you play a sport, you are using Newton's laws of motion.

Take a soccer game, for example. Imagine the ball before kickoff. It is sitting still in the middle of the field. It will never move on its own. The ball will move only if another force acts on it. The force is a player's foot

A ball that is not moving is showing Newton's first law of motion.

kicking the ball. When the player applies force to the ball, it will move.

GRAVITY AND DISTANCE

Gravity gets smaller when things move apart. Earth's gravity is lower in space than on the ground. Things weigh less when gravity gets smaller. Astronauts weigh less in space.

Once the ball is sent flying, what happens? Does it keep moving in a straight line? Does it sail into space? Of course not. But why not? You can't see any forces acting on it. There are unseen forces causing the ball to change speed and direction. If you kick the ball high, air

If it wasn't for the force of gravity, a soccer ball would fly into space when you kick it!

friction will slow it down. Gravity will pull it back to the ground. If you kick the ball along the grass, the friction of the grass will slow it down. It will stop moving. If no one kicks the soccer ball again, it will stay still. All of these things show Newton's first law of motion.

Objects with more weight need more force to move them.

USING NEWTON'S SECOND LAW

Newton's second law of motion is at work in a soccer game, too. The speed of the ball depends on how hard you kick it. If you kick it harder, it will go farther. If you kick it softly, it won't go very far. The change of speed, or the acceleration, also depends on the weight of the ball. If you kick a heavy bowling ball, it won't go as far as a soccer ball. Also, your foot will hurt. A ball's acceleration depends on the size of the ball and the amount of force used to kick it. A soccer star like Cristiano Ronaldo can apply more force to a ball than most kids can.

THE THIRD LAW

Every time you kick a soccer ball you can feel Newton's third law of motion. Here is how it works. When you

The soccer ball will move farther and more quickly if you kick it harder.

apply a force to an object, the object will apply an equal amount of force. That force will be in the opposite direction. When you kick the soccer ball, your leg will send the ball forward. But you can feel the ball as you kick it. This is from the force of the ball pushing against your foot. Heavier balls push back with greater force. Don't kick them. You could break your foot.

Any time you move your body or an object, you put Newton's three laws of motion into action.

THE FIRST LAW

Newton's first law is also called **inertia**. The idea is that objects don't change their motion on their own. An object that is still won't move until something forces it to. A moving object won't stop until something forces it to. A moving object won't change its path unless something forces it to. A pitcher applies force to a ball by throwing it. If you hit the baseball, it will change

FINDING OUT ABOUT FRICTION

Another force that changes the way objects move is friction. Friction happens when one object slides over the surface of something. Here is a way to see friction in action. Make a ramp out of three books. Stack two small books. Lean a bigger book between the floor and the stacked books. Roll a ball down the ramp onto different surfaces. How far does it go? On a smooth tile floor it will travel a long way. The smooth surface creates little friction. Now try it on a carpet or on gravel. On a rough surface it won't travel as far. The rough surface makes more friction.

Friction affects how far a rolling object will travel.

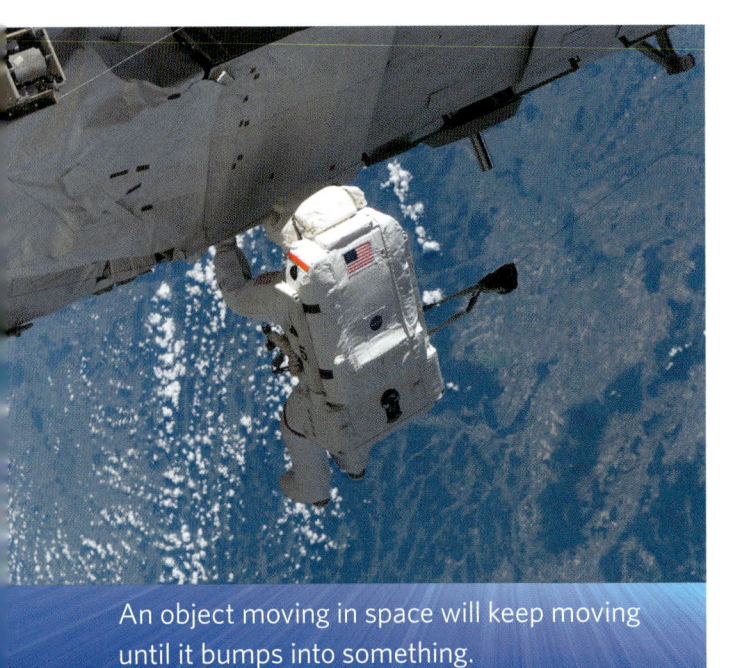
An object moving in space will keep moving until it bumps into something.

direction. If you swing and miss, the catcher's glove will make it stop.

There are several kinds of forces that can act on an object. In Newton's second law, force is defined as a change in **momentum**.

Momentum is a factor of an object's mass and its velocity (or speed). When you kick a soccer ball your foot gives it momentum.

Gravity is a force that can change how objects move. Gravity is an attractive force between two objects. If there was no gravity, every time you threw a ball it would fly into space. It wouldn't stop until some force acted on it.

Some objects can defy the pull of gravity. Newton's third law can be seen in a rocket launch. The rocket thrusters push down from the rocket at the back end. The rocket is pushed up with a force equal to that of the thrusters. It must be pushed up with a force stronger than gravity.

A launching rocket shows Newton's third law of motion.

Ancient Greeks had the same instinctive understanding of physics as we do.

CHAPTER 3

NEW PHYSICS

Sir Isaac Newton stated his three laws more than three hundred years ago. Before then people could predict how objects would move. Kids knew what would happen when they kicked a ball. They just did not know why it would happen.

ARISTOTLE

People believed Aristotle's ideas about motion for centuries before Newton proved them wrong.

Aristotle lived in Greece two thousand years before Newton was alive. He was a philosopher and a scientist. He didn't believe in the idea of inertia. That is Newton's first law. Aristotle believed that an object moved only as long as a force was applied to it. Most people believed him. It would be hundreds of years before Aristotle was proved wrong. Scientists such as Galileo and Nicolaus Copernicus doubted Aristotle. Finally, in 1687, Isaac Newton wrote a book with all of his ideas.

Newton also described gravity, one of the forces that change how objects move.

THE IMPORTANCE OF NEWTON'S LAWS

Newton's laws were the standard for hundreds of years. Then scientists learned new things. Newton's three laws of motion work perfectly for most objects we see every day. They are the ordinary kind of physics

ISAAC NEWTON

Isaac Newton accurately described how objects move.

Isaac Newton (1642–1727) was a scientist who studied many subjects. He studied physics and math. He invented things. He made a new kind of telescope. He studied astronomy. He is one of the most famous scientists in history. Newton identified laws about how objects move. He also figured out how planets and comets move in space. Long ago, many people thought Earth was at the center of the solar system. Newton proved that the sun is at the center. He used his reflecting telescope to do it.

for average life. His laws don't apply under extreme conditions. When an object is moving very fast, the rules change. Things that move close to the speed of light don't follow what is called Newtonian physics.

MODERN PHYSICS

This new physics is called modern physics. Albert Einstein described modern physics. He said that space and time don't always act like we think they do on Earth.

Albert Einstein described how objects move under extreme conditions, such as near the speed of light.

MOVING FAST

Light travels at 186,000 miles (300,000 kilometers) per second. That's 671 million miles per hour (1.08 billion km per hour). Light from Earth reaches the moon in less than one and a half seconds.

Newtonian physics deals with things you can see and touch. It deals with the way things move, such as soccer

Light moves differently than the objects you see every day.

balls and rockets. Modern physics deals with things that are so tiny or so fast that we can't see them. It deals with movement inside atoms. It deals with movement in very high or very low temperatures. It deals with movement at speeds close to the speed of light.

Modern physics also says that the speed of light is a constant. There is no force that can change it. Light doesn't act like an object. Nothing slows it down or speeds it up.

HOW DOES IT MOVE QUIZ

Question 1: *True or false: Mass and weight are the same.*

Question 2: *Which of Newton's three laws deals with inertia?*

Question 3: *What did Isaac Newton invent?*

Answer 1: False. Mass is the amount of matter in an object. It does not change. Weight changes as gravity changes. People weigh less on the moon than on Earth. The moon has less gravity than Earth.

Answer 2: Newton's first law of motion.

Answer 3: He invented a new kind of telescope. It was called a reflecting telescope.

GLOSSARY

acceleration The change in speed over time.

atoms The basic parts of matter. They make up elements. They can also mix to make new elements.

force Something that acts on an object to change its motion.

friction The force that changes movement when one object moves over another.

gravity The attractive force between two objects with mass.

inertia The tendency of an object to continue its motion or to stay still until a force acts on it.

mass The amount of matter in an object.

molecule The smallest part of a substance made up of one or more atoms.

momentum The amount of motion of an object.

physics An area of science that studies matter and energy.

weight A measure of how gravity affects an object.

FIND OUT MORE

BOOKS

Gonick, Larry. *The Cartoon Guide to Physics. New York: HarperPerennial, 1991.*

Pascal, Janet. *Who Was Isaac Newton? New York: Grosset and Dunlap, 2014.*

WEBSITES

Ducksters: Physics for Kids, Laws of Motion

http://www.ducksters.com/science/laws_of_motion.php

The laws of motion are explained with games, stories, and activities. Links are given for other helpful stories.

Rader's Physics4Kids: Motion

http://www.physics4kids.com/files/motion_laws.html

This site has easy-to-understand pages about many aspects of physics, including how objects move.

INDEX

ABOUT THE AUTHOR

Laura L. Sullivan is the author of more than forty fiction and nonfiction books for children, including the fantasies Under the Green Hill and Guardian of the Green Hill. She lives in Florida, where she likes to swim, hike, canoe, hunt fossils, and practice Brazilian jiu jitsu.